Claude
DEBUSSY

PETITE SUITE
Orchestrated by
Henri Büsser
(1907)

SERENISSIMA MUSIC, INC.

INSTRUMENTATION

2 Flutes

2 Oboes

2 Clarinets in B-flat

2 Bassoons

2 Horns in F

2 Trumpets in C

Timpani

Percussion
(Triangle, Cymbals, Tambourine)

Harp

Violin I

Violin II

Viola

Violoncello

Bass

Duration: ca. 13 minutes

ISBN: 1-932419-04-7
ISMN M-800001-04-8

This score is a slightly modified unabridged reprint of the score published in 1908 by Durand et Cie., Paris. The score has been reduced to fit the present format.

Printed in the USA
First Printing: June, 2003

PETITE SUITE

Orchestrée par
HENRI BÜSSER

CLAUDE DEBUSSY

I.— EN BATEAU

SERENISSIMA MUSIC, INC.

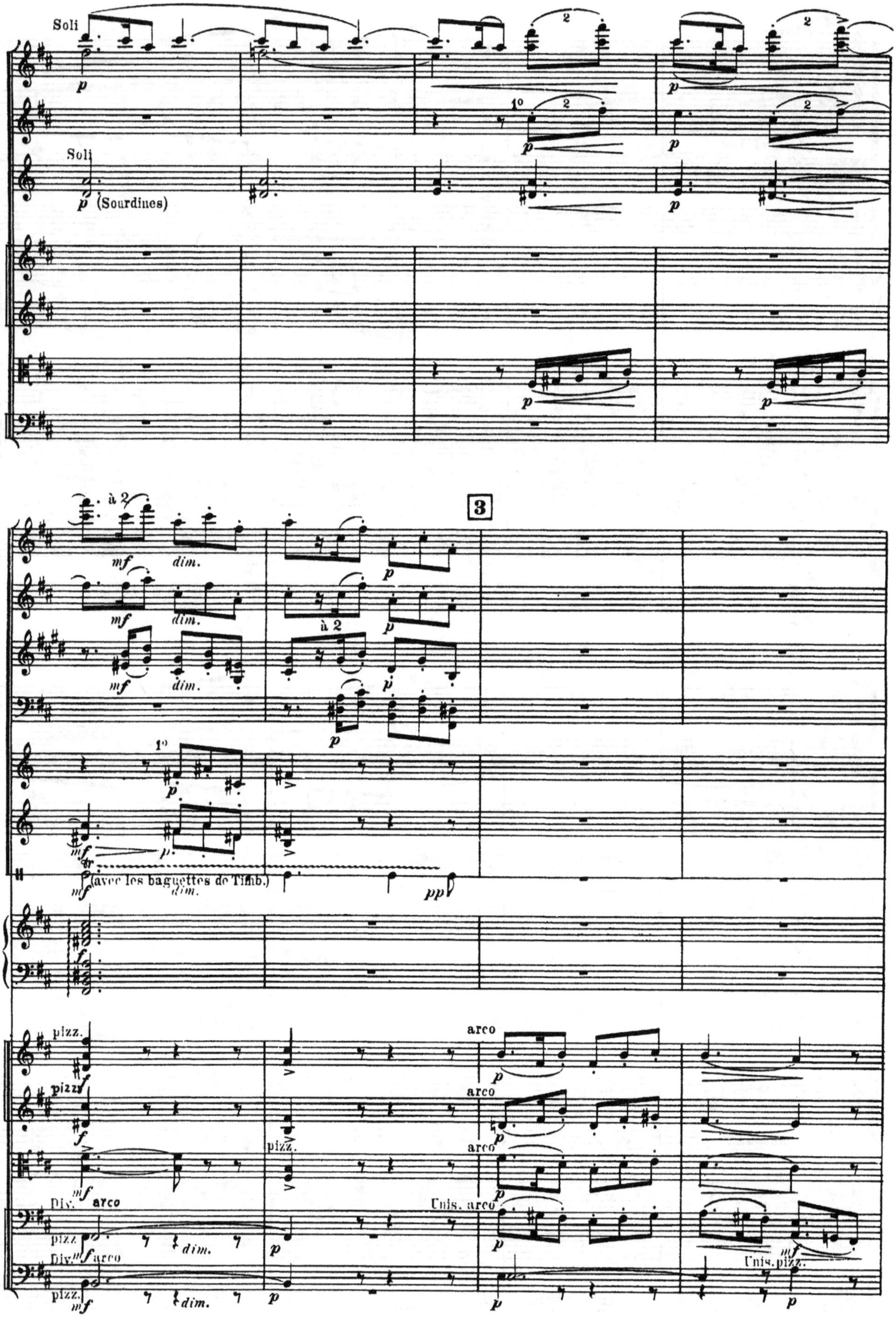
Soli
Soli
(Sourdines)
à 2
3
dim.
(avec les baguettes de Timb.)
pizz.
arco
Div.
Unis. arco
Unis. pizz.

10

12

14

II.—CORTEGE

16

17

18

19

20

22

24

26

29

31

32

33

III.—MENUET

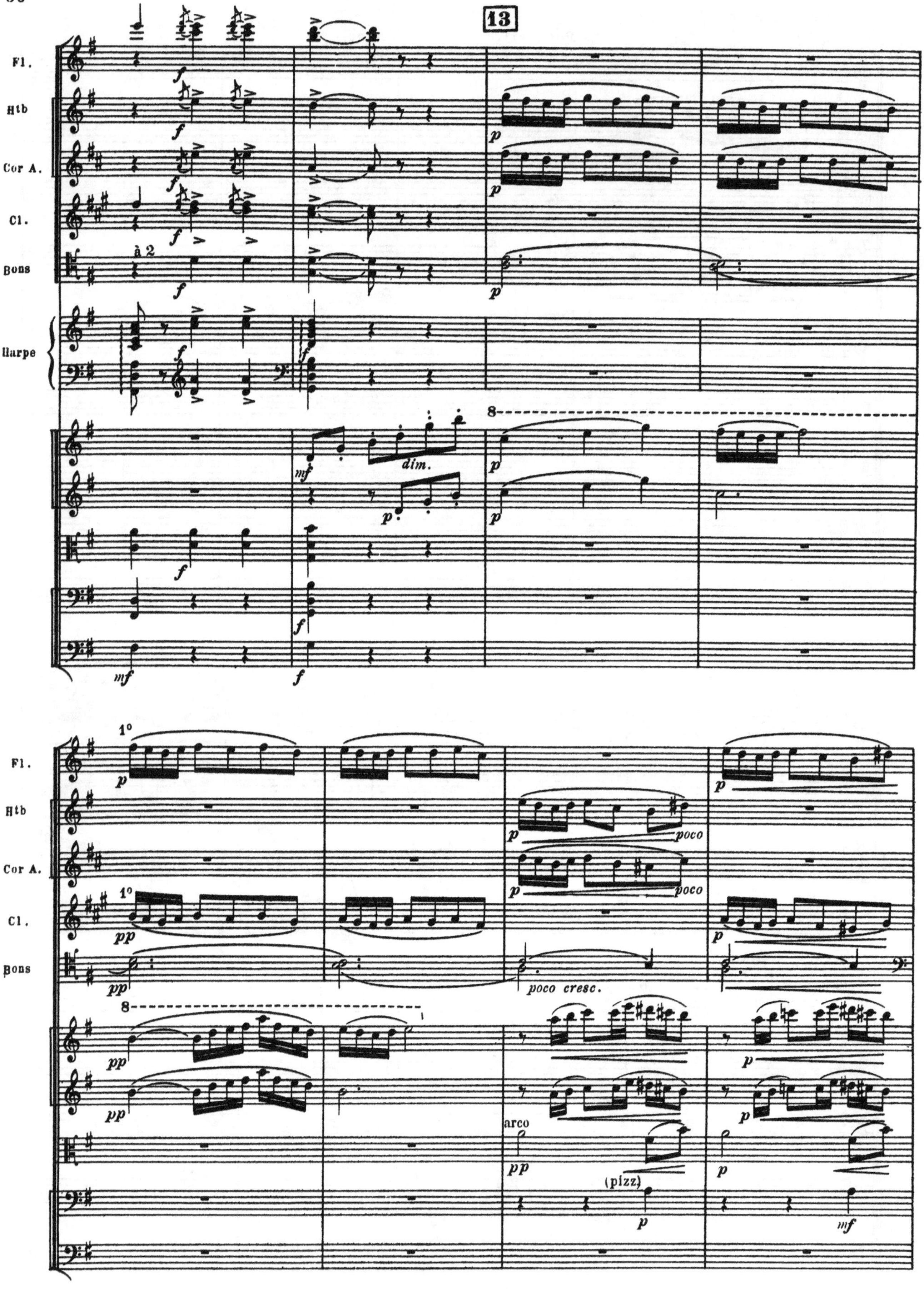
13
Fl.
Htb
Cor A.
Cl.
Bons
à 2
Harpe
dim.
1°
poco
poco cresc.
arco
(pizz)

37

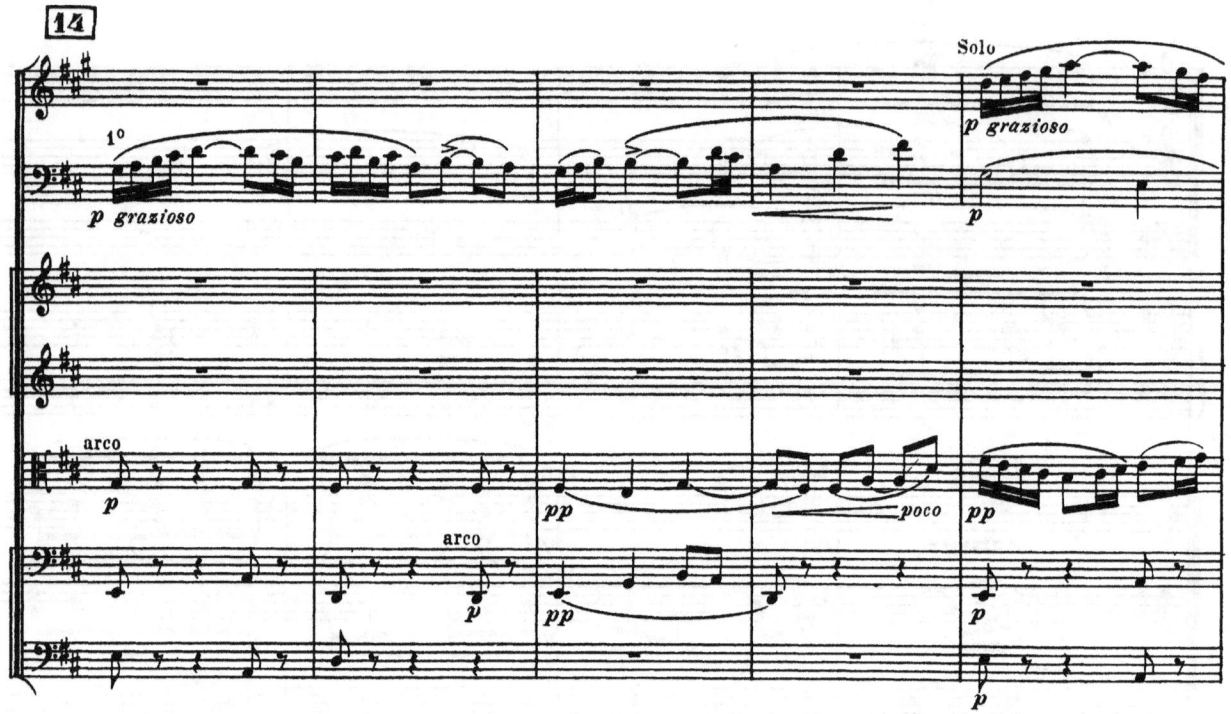

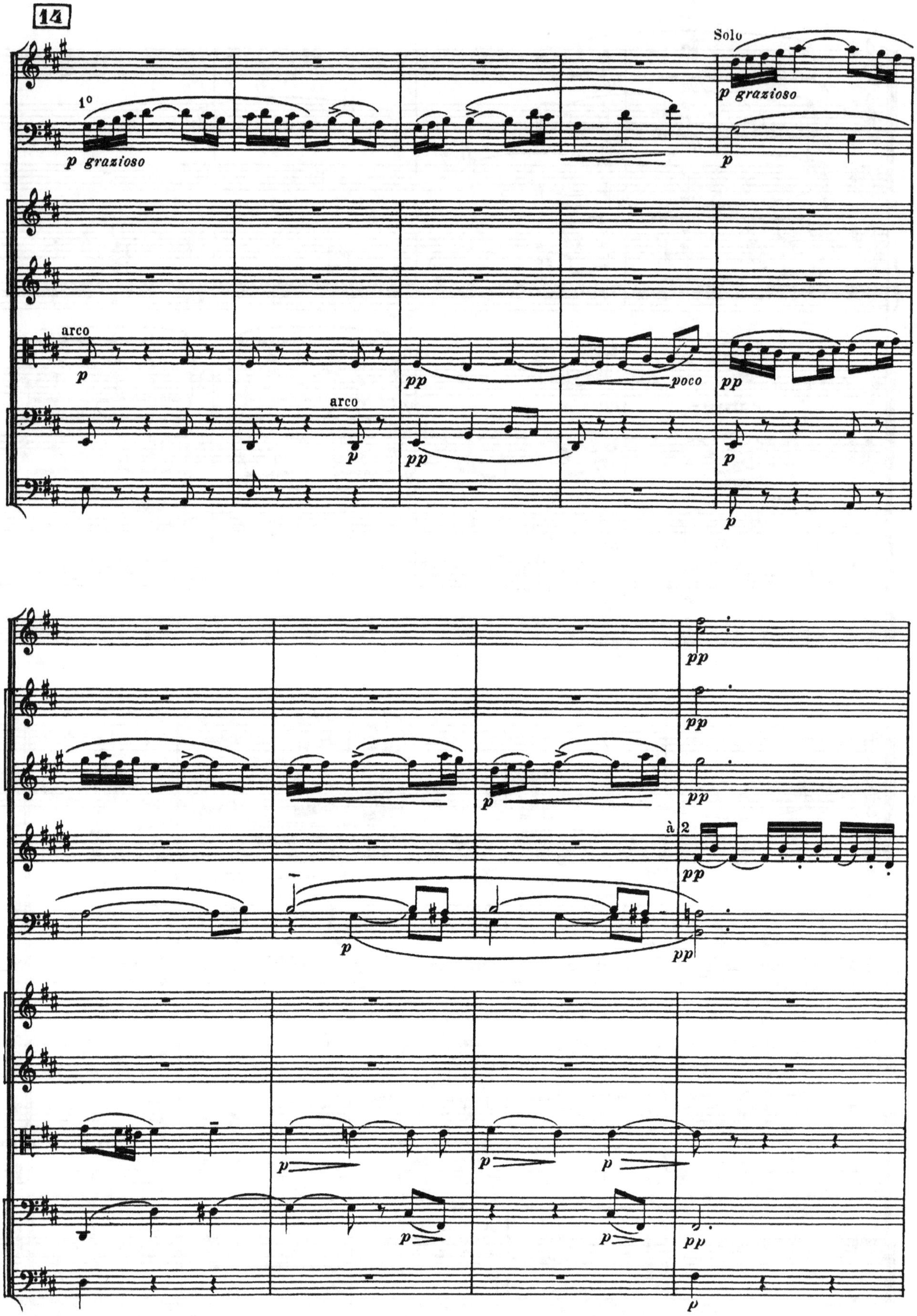
14
Solo
1°
p grazioso
p grazioso
p
arco
p
arco
pp
poco
pp
à 2
pp
p

40

44

IV.— BALLET

48

50

52

55

56

58

64

70

www.ingramcontent.com/pod-product-compliance
Lightning Source LLC
LaVergne TN
LVHW061343060426
835512LV00016B/2646

9781932419047